our wonderful
weather

valerie bodden

tornadoes

our wonderful
weather

Published by Creative Education
P.O. Box 227, Mankato, Minnesota 56002
Creative Education is an imprint of The Creative Company
www.thecreativecompany.us

Design and production by Christine Vanderbeek
Art direction by Rita Marshall
Printed by Corporate Graphics in the United States of America

Photographs by Alamy (J Marshall-Tribaleye Images), Corbis (Chuck Doswell/Visuals Unlimited,
Jim Reed/Science Faction, Jim Reed Photography, Eric Nguyen, Reuters, Visuals Unlimited),
Dreamstime (Greg Blomberg, Jeff Bushelle, Chris White), Getty Images (Philippe Bourseiller,
Nicholas Eveleigh, Johner, Chris Johns/National Geographic, Carsten Peter, Jim Reed, Miami
Herald, Topical Press Agency/Hulton Archive), iStockphoto (Sean Martin, John Murray, Jeff
Smith, Dieter Spears, Clint Spencer, VM)

Library of Congress Cataloging-in-Publication Data

Bodden, Valerie.
Tornadoes / by Valerie Bodden.
Summary: A simple exploration of tornadoes, examining how these spinning storms develop,
how scientists watch for them and measure their strength, and the damage "twisters" can cause.
Includes bibliographical references and index.
ISBN 978-1-60818-150-6
1. Tornadoes—Juvenile literature. I. Title.
QC955.2.B63 2012
551.55'3—dc22   2010053671

CPSIA: 030513 PO1659

4 6 8 9 7 5 3

contents

what is a tornado? 5 • shapes and sizes 8

measuring tornadoes 13 • famous tornadoes 16

funnel in a bottle 22 • glossary 23

read more 24 • web sites 24 • index 24

A tornado is a spinning column of air that reaches from a cloud to the ground. Tornadoes are formed when thunderstorm clouds spin. Sometimes the clouds form a funnel cloud.

Tornadoes start with spinning air high above the ground

If a funnel cloud reaches the ground, it is called a tornado. Tornadoes are sometimes called twisters. Most tornadoes move across the ground at about 30 to 40 miles (48–64 km) per hour.

Funnel clouds and tornadoes are usually a dark gray color

7

Some tornadoes are long and thin. Others are short and wide. The wind in a tornado whips debris (duh-BREE)

wide tornado

through the air. Some tornadoes make a roaring sound like a train. Others sound like a shriek or howl.

Most tornadoes are about 500 yards (457 m) wide. But some can be two miles (3.2 km) across! Strong tornadoes usually stay on the ground for about eight minutes.

The biggest tornadoes can seem to cover the whole sky

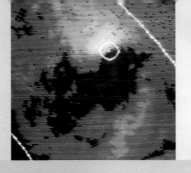

Tornadoes are measured by how fast their winds blow, using a system called the Enhanced Fujita (foo-JEE-tuh) Scale. It is called the EF Scale for short. The weakest tornadoes are called EF0 tornadoes. Their winds blow 65 to 85 miles (105–137 km) per hour. EF5 tornadoes are the strongest, with winds of more than 200 miles (322 km) per hour.

This tornado in Miami, Florida, in 1997 was rated EF1

Meteorologists (mee-tee-uh-RAH-luh-jists) are people who study weather. They try to forecast how the weather

meteorologists

will change. They use radar to see where

spinning storm clouds could form a tornado.

radar truck

On March 18, 1925, the Tri-State Tornado spun through the states of Missouri, Illinois, and Indiana. It was on the ground for more than 3 hours and killed 695 people. During a tornado outbreak on April 3, 1974, almost 150 tornadoes touched down in 13 states in America.

The Tri-State Tornado of 1925 destroyed many houses

flying debris

Tornadoes are very strong and dangerous.

They can tear buildings apart.

18

tornado damage

They can pick up trees and cars. Most of the people who die in tornadoes are hit by flying debris.

If a tornado is spotted on the ground or on radar, meteorologists put out a tornado warning. During a tornado warning, you should go to a basement or a small room with no windows. You do not want to be caught out in one of these powerful storms!

FUNNEL IN A BOTTLE

You can make your own tornado with water. First, fill a two-liter soda bottle about two-thirds full of water. Put an empty two-liter bottle upside down on top of the first bottle. Use duct tape to fasten the two bottles together. Then, tip the bottles over so that the bottle of water is on top. Swirl the water in a circle. Watch as a funnel forms!

GLOSSARY

column — a shape like a tube that is standing up straight

debris — pieces of something that has been broken

forecast — to try to figure out what is going to happen in the future, such as during the next day or week

funnel cloud — a spinning cloud that is shaped like a funnel, or cone, and hangs down from the bottom of a thunderstorm cloud

radar — a system that uses radio waves and computers to measure how far away something (such as a cloud or thunderstorm) is and how fast it is moving

tornado outbreak — the formation of many tornadoes at one time in the same area

READ MORE

Harris, Caroline. *Science Kids: Weather*. London: Kingfisher, 2009.

Wednorff, Anne. *Tornadoes*. Minneapolis: Bellwether Media, 2009.

WEB SITES

FEMA for Kids: Tornadoes

http://www.fema.gov/kids/tornado.htm
Learn more about how to stay safe during a tornado.

National Geographic Kids: Tornadoes

http://kids.nationalgeographic.com/kids/photos/tornadoes/
Check out some wild tornado pictures.

INDEX

clouds   5, 15
debris   8–9, 19
Enhanced Fujita Scale   13
funnel clouds   5, 6
meteorologists   14–15, 21
radar   15
size   10

sound   9
speed   6
thunderstorms   5
tornado outbreaks   16
tornado warnings   21
Tri-State Tornado   16
wind   8–9, 13